Pooh

Photograph of Baby

First published in Great Britain in 1997
by Methuen Children's Books
an imprint of Egmont Children's Books Limited
Michelin House, 81 Fulham Road, London SW3 6RB
Copyright © 1997 Michael John Brown, Peter Janson-Smith
Roger Hugh Vaughan Charles Morgan and
Timothy Michael Robinson, Trustees of the Pooh Properties.
From Winnie-the-Pooh, first published 1926,
The House at Pooh Corner, first published 1928,
and Now We Are Six, first published 1927
Text by A.A.Milne and line drawings by E.H.Shepard
copyright under the Berne Convention.
Colouring of the line illustrations from Winnie-the-Pooh and The House at Pooh Corner
copyright © 1973, 1974 Ernest H. Shepard
and Methuen Children's Books Limited.
Colouring of the line illustrations from Now We Are Six by Mark Burgess
copyright © 1989 Egmont Children's Books Limited.
Design copyright © 1997 Egmont Children's Books Limited.

7 9 10 8 6

ISBN 0416 19352 8

Printed in Belgium

Winnie~the~Pooh
Baby Days

with texts by A.A.Milne

illustrations by E.H.Shepard

Methuen Children's Books

Contents

Waiting for Baby 8

Baby's Birth 10

Things to Remember 12

Coming Home 14

Settling Down 15

Naming Baby 16

Family Tree 18

Baby's Progress 20

Bathtime 22

Bedtime 23

Mealtimes 24

Baby's Health 26

Teething 27

Growing 28

Going Out 30

First Holiday 31

First Christmas 32

First Birthday 34

Taking Steps 36

First Words 37

First Events 38

Favourite Things 40

Special Memories 42

The Future 44

Waiting for Baby

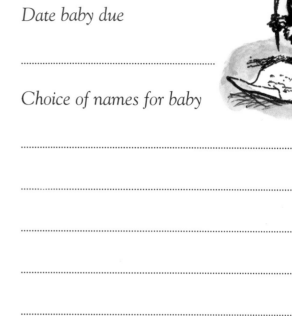

Date baby due

....

Choice of names for baby

....

....

....

....

....

Mother's name

....

Father's name

....

How Mother and Father met

....

....

....

....

Prenatal scan   Date..

Now it happened that Kanga had felt rather motherly that morning, and Wanting to Count Things – like Roo's vests, and how many pieces of soap there were left , and the two clean spots in Tigger's feeder; so she sent them out with a packet of watercress sandwiches and a packet of extract-of-malt sandwiches for Tigger.

Feelings about having a baby

....

....

....

....

....

When I first heard his name, I said, just as
you are going to say, "But I thought he was a boy?"
"So did I," said Christopher Robin.
"Then you can't call him Winnie?"
"I don't."
"But you said —"
"He's Winnie-ther-Pooh.
Don't you know what 'ther' means?"

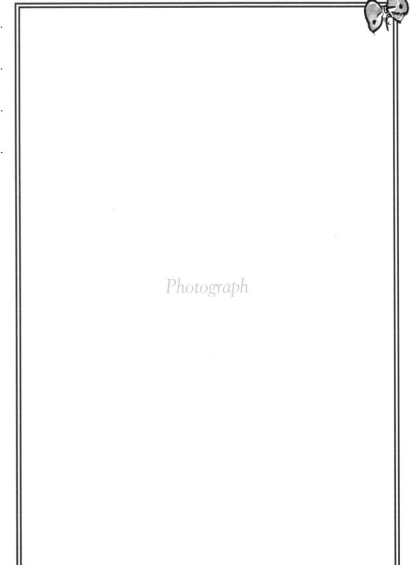

Photograph

Mother/Father

Baby was born on　　　day　　　month　　　year

....

Time of birth

....

Place of birth

....

Who was present at the birth

....

"When you wake up in the morning, Pooh," said Piglet at last, "what's the first thing you say to yourself?"
"What's for breakfast?" said Pooh.
"What do you say, Piglet?"
"I say, I wonder what's going to happen exciting today?" said Piglet.
Pooh nodded thoughtfully.
"It's the same thing," he said.

Weight at birth

....

Length at birth

....

Colour of eyes

....

Colour of hair

....

Name of midwife

....

Name of doctor

....

Description of the birth

....

....

....

....

....

....

....

....

....

Photograph

Very first photograph of baby

Identity tag from hospital

Handprint

Footprint

"I think –" began Piglet nervously.
"Don't," said Eeyore.
"I think Violets *are* rather nice,"
said Piglet. And he laid his bunch in
front of Eeyore and scampered off.

Pressed flowers

Visitors

....

....

....

....

....

Who sent flowers

....

....

....

....

....

Cards and gifts from   Date

....

....

....

Baby came home on

....

Address of family home

....

....

....

Who was there to welcome baby?

....

....

....

On the first night home baby fell asleep at

.... am/pm

.... am/pm

Baby woke at

.... am/pm

.... am/pm

Photograph

Baby's first night at home

Settling Down

Baby's feeding times

....

....

Breast or bottle?

....

Sleeping times

....

Wakeful times

....

Favourite sleeping position

....

Then Tigger looked up at the ceiling, and closed his eyes, and his tongue went round and round his chops, in case he had left any outside, and a peaceful smile came over his face as he said, "So that's what Tiggers like!"

Mother's feelings

....

....

....

Father's feelings

....

....

....

Naming Baby

Pooh

Now this bear's name is Winnie, which shows what a good name for bears it is, but the funny thing is that we can't remember whether Winnie is called after Pooh, or Pooh after Winnie. We did know once, but we have forgotten.

Baby's name

....

Date of Christening or Name Day celebrations

....

Baby wore

....

Godparents

....

....

....

Photograph

Baby's Day

Piglit

Baby's name means

....

Name was chosen by

....

Reason for choosing name

....

....

Gifts received

....

....

....

....

....

....

....

Photograph

The Celebrations

Family Tree

Family Photograph

Next to his house was a piece of broken board which had:
"TRESPASSERS W" on it. When Christopher Robin asked
the Piglet what it meant, he said it was his grandfather's
name, and had been in the family for a long time.

Mother's side

Great Grandmother

....

Great Grandfather

....

Grandmother

....

Grandfather

....

Baby's Mother

....

Father's side

Great Grandmother

....

Great Grandfather

....

Grandmother

....

Grandfather

....

Baby's Father

....

Baby's Sisters

....

....

....

Baby's Brothers

....

....

....

Baby's Progress

Photograph

Date ....

Wakes up at

....

Bathtime

....

Mealtimes

....

....

....

Goes to sleep at

....

Sometimes Winnie-the-Pooh likes a game of some sort when he comes downstairs, and sometimes he likes to sit quietly in front of the fire and listen to a story …

How baby has changed

....
....
....
....
....

Favourite activities

....
....
....
....
....

Describe baby's first weeks

....
....
....
....
....

Does baby like bathtime?

....

Favourite bath toys

....

Favourite bath games

....

....

First bath at home

....

First time in the big bath

....

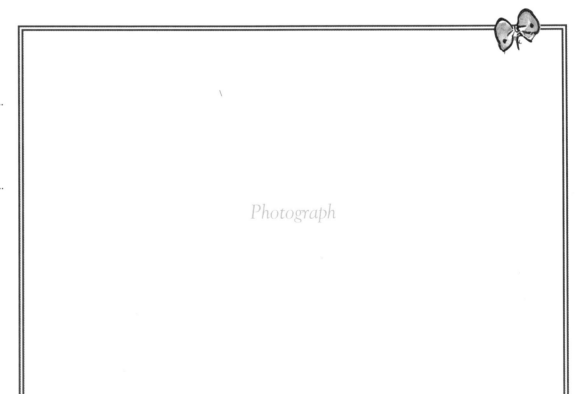

Photograph

Baby's bathtime

Sleeping times

....

....

First slept through the night

....

Moved to a cot

....

....

Favourite bedtime toys

....

....

Favourite bedtime stories

....

....

Favourite lullabies

....

....

Binker's brave as lions when we're running in the park;
Binker's brave as tigers when we're lying in the dark;
Binker's brave as elephants. He never, never cries …
Except (like other people) when the soap gets in his eyes.

Mealtimes

Weaned from the breast/bottle on

....

Date baby first:

Ate puréed food

....

Ate solid food

....

Used fingers

....

Held a spoon

....

Sat in a high chair

....

Drank from a cup with help

....

Drank from a cup alone

....

Ate a complete meal

....

Pooh put the cloth back on the table, and he put a large honey-pot on the cloth, and they sat down to breakfast. And as soon as they sat down, Tigger took a large mouthful of honey ... and he looked up at the ceiling with his head on one side, and made exploring noises with his tongue, and considering noises, and what-have-we-got-here noises ... and then he said in a very decided voice: "Tiggers don't like honey."

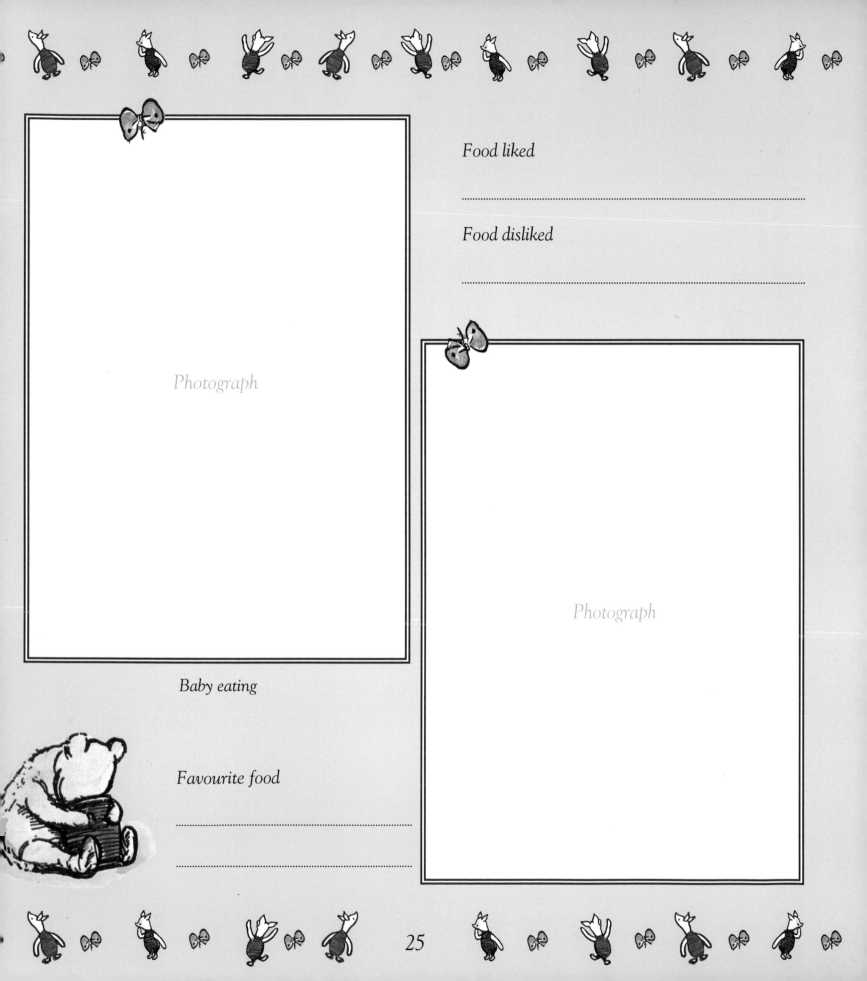

Food liked

....

Food disliked

....

Photograph

Photograph

Baby eating

Favourite food

....

Baby's Health

Immunization details

Vaccine	Age	Date
Diphtheria		....
Tetanus		....
Whooping cough		....
Polio		....
Meningitis		....

Eyesight test

....

Hearing test

....

Childhood illnesses	Date
....	....
....	....
....	....

Allergies

....

Blood group

....

Local doctor

....

Telephone number

....

"I don't think Roo had better come," he said. "Not today."
"Why not?" said Roo, who wasn't supposed to be listening.
"Nasty cold day," said Rabbit, shaking his head. " And you were coughing this morning."
"How do you know?" asked Roo indignantly.
"Oh, Roo, you never told me," said Kanga reproachfully.
"It was a biscuit cough," said Roo, "not one you tell about."

A baby cuts 20 primary or milk teeth from about six months old to two years old. The appearance of the first tooth is a milestone in a baby's life, although it can cause a great deal of discomfort. Some babies find chewing on a teething ring soothes the gums and helps lessen the pain. These first milk teeth begin to be replaced with permanent teeth when the child is about six years old.

Date of first tooth

....

Date of second tooth

....

Date of third tooth

....

Date of fourth tooth

....

Date of fifth tooth

....

Date of sixth tooth

....

Date of seventh tooth

....

Date of eighth tooth

....

Date of ninth tooth

....

Date of tenth tooth

....

Binker isn't greedy, but he does like things to eat,
So I have to say to people when they're giving me a sweet,
"Oh, Binker wants a chocolate, so could you give me two?"
And then I eat it for him, 'cos his teeth are rather new.

Growing

Age	Weight	Length/Height
One month	....	....
Two months	....	....
Three months	....	....
Four months	....	....
Five months	....	....
Six months	....	....
Seven months	....	....
Eight months	....	....
Nine months	....	....
Ten months	....	....
Eleven months	....	....
Twelve months	....	....

What shall we do about poor little Tigger?
If he never eats nothing he'll never get bigger.
But whatever his weight in pounds, shillings and ounces,
He always seems bigger because of his bounces.

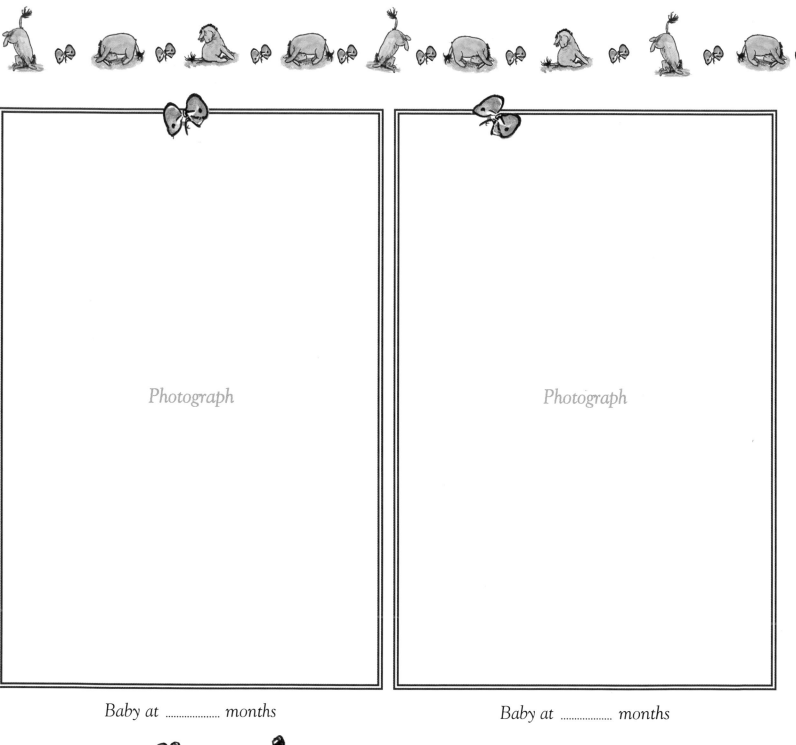

Photograph

Photograph

Baby at .... months

Baby at .... months

"He's quite big enough anyhow," said Piglet.
"He isn't really very big."
"Well he seems so."

Going Out

First outing in *pram/push chair*

....

First outings made by

Car ....

Train ....

Bus ....

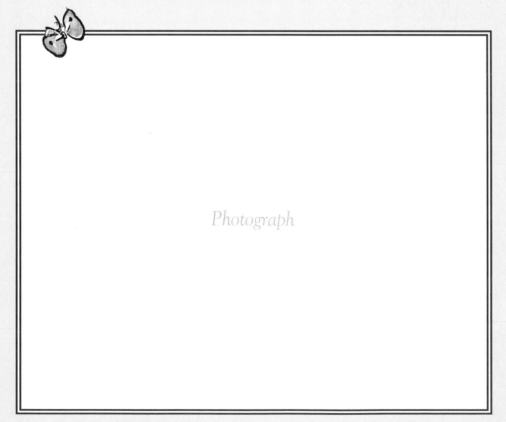

Photograph

Baby on an outing to ....

Special outings with

Grandparents

....

....

Relatives

....

....

Friends

....

....

First Holiday

First holiday

....

Travelled by

....

Where it was spent

....

Favourite activity

....

Favourite outings

....

....

"Christopher Robin and I are going for a Short Walk,"
he said, "not a Jostle. If he likes to bring Pooh and Piglet
with him, I shall be glad of their company, but one must
be able to Breathe."

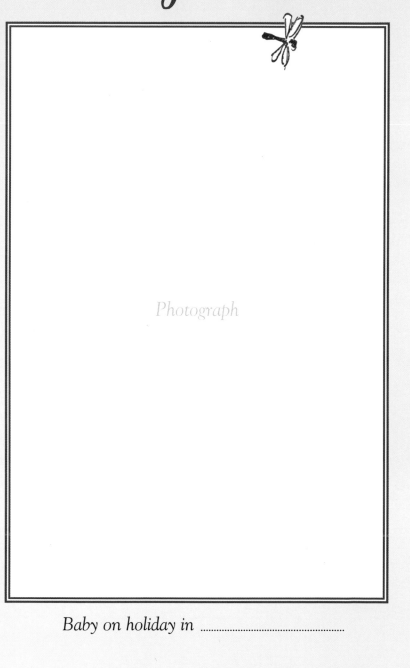

Photograph

Baby on holiday in ....

Favourite memories of the holiday

....

....

First Christmas

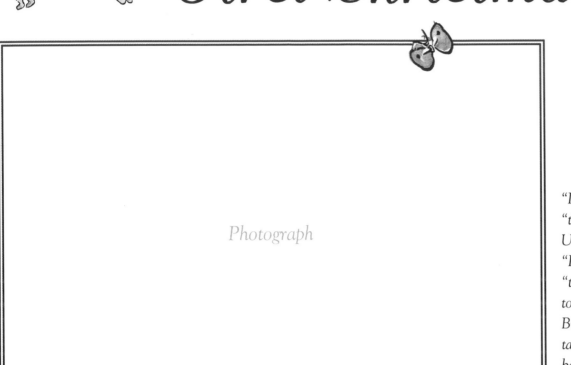

Photograph

Baby's first Christmas

"I'm very glad," said Pooh happily,
"that I thought of giving you a
Useful Pot to put things in."
"I'm very glad," said Piglet happily,
"that I thought of giving you Something
to put in a Useful Pot."
But Eeyore wasn't listening. He was
taking the balloon out, and putting it
back again, as happy as could be …

Description of Christmas Day

....

....

....

Who it was spent with

Where it was spent

....

....

....

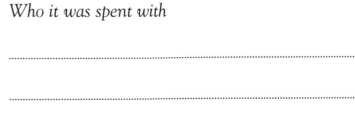

Where Boxing Day was spent

....

Who it was spent with

....

....

....

Your present to baby

....

Description of Boxing Day

....

Stocking gifts

....

....

....

....

Gifts received   from

....

....

....

....

....

First Birthday

Date

....

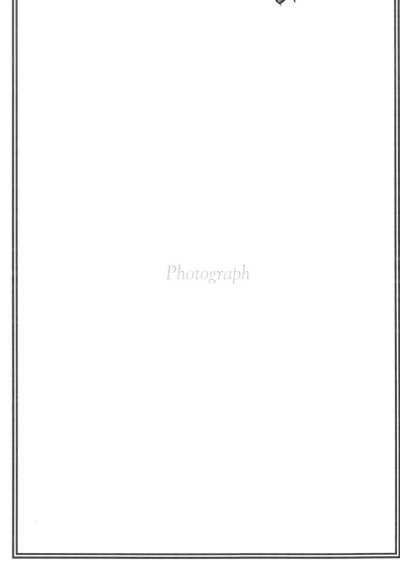

Photograph

How it was celebrated

....

....

....

Who was there

....

....

....

First birthday

Where it was spent

....

Description of cake

....

....

What did baby wear?

....

....

Gifts received   from

....

....

....

....

Piglet had gone back to his own house to get Eeyore's balloon. He held it very tightly against himself, so that it shouldn't blow away, and he ran as fast as he could so as to get to Eeyore before Pooh did; for he thought that he would like to be the first one to give a present, just as if he had thought of it without being told by anybody.

Your present

....

Taking Steps

Photograph

Photograph

Crawling   Date..

Holding on   Date..

Photograph

Photograph

Standing up   Date..

First steps without help   Date..

First Words

First Sounds .... Date .... Favourite books

....

....

....

First Words

....

....

....

Binker's always talking, 'cos I'm teaching him to speak:
He sometimes likes to do it in a funny sort of squeak,
And he sometimes likes to do it in a hoodling sort of roar …
And I have to do it for him 'cos his throat is rather sore.

Focused eyes

....

Smiled

....

Sucked thumb or dummy

....

Slept through the night

....

Held head up

....

Played with hands

....

Played with feet

....

Clapped hands

....

Grasped an object

....

O Timothy Tim
  Has ten pink toes,
  And ten pink toes
Has Timothy Tim.
They go with him
  Wherever he goes,
  And wherever he goes
They go with him.

O Timothy Tim
  Has two blue eyes,
  And two blue eyes
Has Timothy Tim.
They cry with him
  Whenever he cries,
  And whenever he cries,
They cry with him.

Gurgled

....

Laughed

....

Said ma-ma

....

Said da-da

....

Spoke first words

....

Made animal noises

....

Rolled right over

....

Sat up

....

Started to crawl

....

Pulled him/herself upright

....

Stood alone

....

Took first steps with help

....

Took first steps alone

....

Started climbing

....

Wore shoes

....

Walked outside

....

Waved goodbye

....

Had a haircut

....

First baby-sitter

....

Recognised his/her name

....

Ate solid food

....

Drank from a cup

....

Used a spoon

....

Cut a tooth

....

First kiss

....

Favourite Things

Baby's favourite:

Mobile

....

Games

....

....

Activities

....

....

Songs and nursery rhymes

....

....

Pictures

....

....

Toys

....

....

Books

....

....

Cuddly toys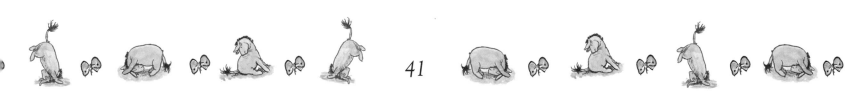

....

....

People

....

....

....

Animals

....

....

Sounds

....

....

Music

....

....

"What do you like doing best in the world, Pooh?"
"Well," said Pooh, "what I like best –" and then he had to stop and think.
Because although Eating Honey was a very good thing to do, there was a
moment just before you began to eat it which was better than when you were,
but he didn't know what it was called. And then he thought that being with
Christopher Robin was a very good thing to do, and having Piglet near was
a very friendly thing to have.

What makes baby laugh

....

....

....

....

Special Memories

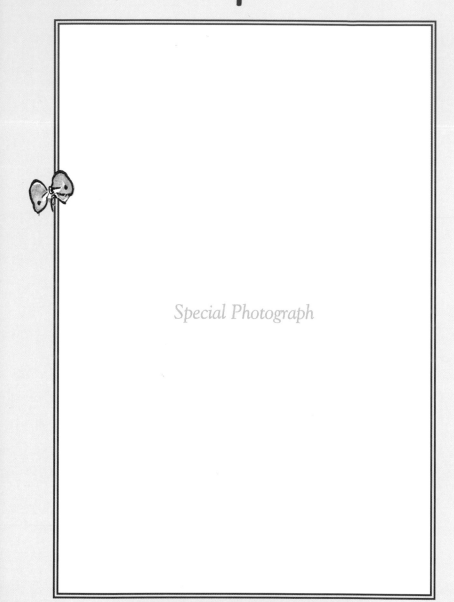

Special Photograph

Date ....

"Oh, Bear!" said Christopher Robin.
"How I do love you!"
"So do I," said Pooh.

Looking back on the first year of your baby's life
you may like to record some special moments.

First friends

....
....
....

Special things to remember

....
....
....
....
....
....

Funny ways

....

....

....

....

....

Photograph

Baby's friends

The Future

Plans for the future

....

....

....

"Do you know what A means, little Piglet?"
"No, Eeyore, I don't."
"It means Learning, it means Education, it means all the things that you and Pooh haven't got. That's what A means."
"Oh," said Piglet again. "I mean, does it?" he explained very quickly.

Possible nursery schools

....

....

....

....

Baby's character

....

....

....

....

....

....